A PG-13 Literary Magazine for readers of Young Adult Fiction

Fall 2015
Volume 3 Issue 2

Editor-Nichole Hansen
Editor-Tevin Hansen
Cover Art-Monica Adrian

Stinkwaves Magazine
www.stinkwavesmagazine.com
submissions@stinkwavesmagazine.com

Because adults don't give out stinkwaves . . .
only children do that.

-Roald Dahl, *The Witches*

Stinkwaves Magazine Fall 2015

Handersen Publishing

WHat's INSide

What's Inside Cont.

Featured Artists in this Issue

Monica Adrian

      Witchhhh (Cover)

Elle Alexander

      Grimly Jane (8)

Jay Duret

      Dark Spaces (27), Headwinds (60)

Don Ford

      Swamp Creature (29)

Jane Gregoritch

      The Cat Who Broke the Witch's Heart (32-50)

Tevin Hansen

      Mummy Mouse (5), Worm of Wisdom (54)

Molly Satterthwaite

      Seasonal Greeting (18), Blood or Chocolate (30)

Sephonē Zorro

      The Cat Who Broke the Witch's Heart (32-50)

FroM tHe StoryteLLer GuY

The scariest stories of all are always *true* stories. Not urban myths, but actual true events. And the following story actually happened. In fact, this may be the scariest TRUE story you've ever read in your whole life. It is the story of a terrifying, tyrannical mouse that was so very close to taking over the world by draining our life-forces, one at a time, house by house, town by town.

You can thank my wife for saving mankind.

However, she was also the person responsible for actually *creating* this monster. The vicious, dreaded, evil creature known simply as…MUMMY MOUSE.

Back in 2007, my wife and I had just purchased our first home. It was a nice two bedroom/one bath house with a really cool add-on, which nearly doubled the size of the house. The add-on was almost like having our own private ski lodge, with huge windows, a 16-foot ceiling, and a spectacular view (…of the backyard, not mountains).

First you travelled through the (rather small) kitchen, down three carpeted steps, then into a wide open space. Our "lodge" had a fireplace, room for several couches, a couple recliners, and it also served as my wife's painting area, quilting area, and still had room left over for a computer—my writing room. (Fortunately, I came to my senses and took over the 2nd bedroom. There were no kids back then, so my writing room was huge! Oh, the good old days…)

1

At the far end of our living room was a heavy wooden door that led into the backyard. This door weighed, I swear, approximately fifteen hundred pounds—a big beast of a door with a large weather seal around its entirety, to keep the cold out during those frigid Midwest winters.

Unfortunately, due to being improperly installed (or perhaps the house "settling") the gap underneath the door was approximately 3/4 of an inch. This, of course, was the perfect height for mice to sneak through. The mice could basically waltz on in without even bumping their heads.

So, of course they did.

Not too many at first. But after one mouse comes in, looks around, maybe picks up a few crumbs here and there…the next thing you know he's told all his mouse friends, and soon your house is the place to be.

My favorite part of the story is how tough my wife acted when these furry little creepy-crawlers began to invade our new home. I asked her if she was frightened of the creatures commonly called *Mus Muculus*.

"Mice?" she said, *obviously* no stranger to the scientific name for field mice. "No problem! They don't bother me one bit."

Then I caught one in a mouse trap (the catch-and-release kind) and she couldn't go near it. She waited until I got home, and the moment I came through the front door, I got: "There's a mouse in the trap. Get rid of it. *NOOOOOW!!!!*"

(At least that's how I remember it…)

Genius that I am, I simply took all these mice I caught to the far end of our (reasonably lengthy) backyard, and then released them.

Again and again I did this, week after week. So, yes, I probably ended up catching and releasing the same mouse on more than one occasion. And, mercifully, the mice eventually took the hint and stopped bothering us.

All except one mouse.

After the mouse problem seemed to have taken care of itself, one mouse kept coming around when all the others had stopped. I never actually *saw* him…only his shadow as he hurried across the living room carpet, ignoring the traps I set for him, sniffing but never eating the cheese, peanut butter, or whatever tasty treat I put in there for him.

He was not Mummy Mouse—not yet. Not until my wife decided to take things into her hands. And, honestly, I can't blame her, since I was spending way too much money on mouse traps for this one little critter that wouldn't go away. This particular mouse did not fall for the mouse traps I laid out for him, day after day, night after night. I'd purchased every single kind of mouse trap I could get my hands on, and none of them worked.

We also had some mouse *poison.*

There was an entire box of it in the garage. Neither one of us actually remembered buying mouse poison, so it was possibly left behind by the previous owners. Either way, my wife decided to test it out, because no matter what *I* tried, I couldn't catch that devious little mouse.

Even though the box clearly stated "…just a few pellets will rid your house of mice…" my wife proceeded to dump the entire contents of the box onto a plate. She set it in the closet next to the back door then promptly forgot about it for the next *three weeks.*

Oh, that poor little mouse.

Over the course of the next few weeks, that once cute, lively, furry little guy rotted, shriveled, and finally became mummified.

Unfortunately, I wasn't there when my wife went into the closet and picked up the plate with the withered mouse corpse on it.

I received this text: "It touched me."

Obviously, I had no idea what my wife was talking about. When I got home that night, I heard all about how she picked up the plate with the poison on it, and didn't even *see* the withered, mummified mouse corpse lying there…at least not until it jumped at her, seeking his revenge.

Then I laughed. Oh, how I laughed.

But that event got me thinking how the idea of a "mummy mouse" might make a good short story. The "red eyes" popped into my head, the draining of life-forces, etc…

And hence, Mummy Mouse lives on.

And on…

So if you hear the sound of teeny tiny footsteps scraping across the kitchen floor in the dead of night…*run*. Don't pack, don't collect your sentimental belongings, just get out of the house. Mummy Mouse is probably dragging his dead, rotted, mummified corpse towards your bedroom.

Guard your life-force, everyone.

The Storyteller Guy.

PS--Enjoy the issue!

Mummy Mouse—Tevin Hansen

The Laughing Web

Monica Adrian

One dark Halloween night,

Two girls were in for a fright,

They heard a rumor of a witch with a frosty glare,

She was blind in both eyes with a deathly stare,

The two girls set out to visit this witch,

They felt an urge within them like an itch,

So they made their way up the thorny hill,

And many times were they pricked and blood did they spill,

They finally made their way to the door and three times did they knock,

But then they realized the door was unlocked,

So they looked at each other before coming in,

To see the witch and oh how she was thin,

The witch eerily said, "I've awaited your arrival,"

The girls were scared and questioned their survival,

They turned around and tried to run,

But the witch stopped them in a web she magically spun,

"No don't go," she begged them to stay,

But the girls were determined to get away,

They squirmed and they desperately wriggled,

But all of a sudden they started to giggle,

The witch got upset to see them laughing in glee,

"Stop it!" she said, "Aren't you scared of me?"

But the girls could not cease their laughter,

And in the web they lived happily after,

The witch didn't realize that in making that web she had cast,

A spell to make children's laughter endlessly last,

In time the children died of chill,

Now, new children come to visit and hear the laughter still.

Grimly Jane—Elle Alexander

The Witch in Albert's Back Yard

Scáth Beorh

I had never seen a witch grow as a fruit tree, but Albert bet me my *Strange Worlds #1* that he had one growing in his back yard. It was a warm February weekend day, all my chores were done to dad's approval, and Albert's mom was feeding us Sloppy Joes—my fave.

The witch shook her skinny citrus limbs when we got near her. Six more dead leaves dropped off. I watched them swirl to the grass. I imagined they were disguised spacecraft landing on the green surface of Saturn.

"I fed her tuna fish last night like I do with all the stray cats around here," Albert said. Then he shrugged his shoulders like he didn't know if that was the right thing to do or not.

"I don't think you should'a done that," I said. "Now she's gonna want baked fish. And French fries. And some of your mom's blackberry pie. I think you might'a started something you can't stop."

"Aww, I dunno. She can't move from where she's growing. She don't even talk loud. Listen to her whisper."

I cocked my good ear toward the tree. I could hear a breeze blowing, but I didn't hear the witch say a word. "I can't hear nothing," I said. I was really interested, though, because Albert had never lied to me or even tricked me all our lives, and we had been best friends since we were one or two years old. I didn't care if I lost my comic book in the bet, but I needed solid proof first.

"Go get some more tuna fish."

"We're all out. I gave her the last can."

"Then get some deviled ham or something."

"Let's just wait until we eat lunch and then we'll give her some of our Sloppy Joes, what'cha say?"

"Oh alright," I said, disappointed. "Let's get to work on them vampire kits."

We left the witch growing there where she stood and traipsed out to the shed in the far back corner of Albert's yard. All the neighborhood kids liked our Vampire Hunter Kits. We sold lots of them around Halloween every year.

My mom gave me and Albert some of her quilting cloth and other kinds of cloth and showed us how to sew drawstring bags. We had to make the bags pretty big because we had to fit three cloves of garlic strung together, a bottle of holy tap water, another bottle filled with holy cooking oil, a wooden stake big enough to puncture a vampire's heart, a page from the Bible, and a Cross of Jesus made out of two sticks tied together—mallets sold separately at Jemison's Hardware, and a dime dropped in by the vampire hunter if he wanted some silver in there.

One day Bick Fidelio asked us if we had 'Ghoul Defense Packs' or something like that, and then all the other kids thought we had those too, and everybody started asking for them. But when me and Albert had our next tree-house meeting, we talked it over, and it didn't make any sense to us because ghouls dig up graves and mess around with dead people, and the kids who were asking for the ghoul kits weren't dead yet, and were less likely to be dead if they hurried up and bought our Vampire Hunter Kits. So that's what we started saying whenever somebody asked for things to protect them from ghouls and other kinds of monsters. We sold a lot more vampire kits that way. I watched my comic collection grow by the day, and dad watched my cavities grow by the week.

We made seven more Vampire Hunter Kits that afternoon before Albert's mom called us in to eat. She was a nice lady. She gave us Sloppy Joes with kosher dill pickles and iced tea, sweetened with honey, I think. Oh, yeah, and potato chips.

"Nothing sugary today," she said with a big smile. "Albert's got too many tooth cavities already." I thought that Albert's dad must've really liked his wife's smile.

I saved three pinches of my third Sloppy Joe, and Albert did the same thing. We dropped them into a paper lunch bag. Then I rolled it up and stuck it in the back of my pants under my shirt, which had come untucked anyway. After all, it was Saturday. It'd be tucked in for church the next day anyway, and for school all week. One afternoon wasn't going to hurt anything.

"Hear her?" said Albert as he grabbed my head and turned it in the direction of the witch.

"No."

"Oh c'mon, Rolly!"

"I really can't hear her…*wait…*"

"Yeah?"

"I hear something!"

The breeze had picked up while we were inside eating, and I saw it rustling through all the trees and bushes.

"You hear that?" said Albert, stepping closer to the witch.

"Don't get too close! She might grab you and pull you underground! I read one time about a man who lived in the woods and he trapped kids by leaving treasure for them to find, and when they did find it he came out from behind a tree and pulled them underground and ate them alive! *Stop. Albert!* That's close enough! *Stop!*"

Albert stopped inching forward toward the witch tree. "Hear that?" he said.

"Not sure…" I felt cold sweat bead up on my forehead.

"She said 'hungry!' I heard it, Rolly. She says she's hungry."

"Yeah, for two twelve year old boys! Get away from her!"

But Albert got too close, and the witch grabbed him and pulled him into her scrawny limbs. "Help! *Rolly!*"

"I'll get you out!" I said as I snatched the bag of Sloppy Joe pieces out of my belt, snapped it open, and flung the food at the monster. One piece slapped Albert upside the face and slid down into his mouth that was open in a silent scream of terror. He coughed and choked…and chewed. "Yum," he said, but his heart just wasn't in it. The rest of the pieces flew into the witch's branches and then plopped down around her roots like hot lava out of a volcano or something.

"Too bad our Vampire Hunter Kit won't work on witches!" I said as I looked over at the pile of kits we had made. "Maybe we should've made Anti-Witch Potion!"

"G-garlic! C-cross, Rolly!" said Albert as a twig found his mouth and started diving down his throat. "B-bible! H-h-holy w-water!"

Man, was I stupid! Of course a witch would be afraid of holy oil and holy water! I ran and got one of our kits and ripped it open. "*Albert, hang on hang on hang on!*"

The Bible page made the twig pop back out of his throat, but now other twigs and branches were doing all kinds of mean things to my friend. I slung holy water and holy oil and garlic cloves and more garlic cloves! "Take that, you stupid witch tree! See if I don't cut you down here in a minute after I get my buddy outta there!" I whipped the Cross of Jesus out and danced around the tree reciting Psalm 23 and the Lord's Prayer back to back, over and over until Albert slid, unconscious, to the ground. The last dead leaf of the witch fell off her and did its slow flight to the grass. I pulled my friend away from her roots and checked his pulse. He was still alive, but barely. Then I went and got the axe out of the shed. I made short work of that witch and then, with the help of some kerosene, made a fire with her to warm Albert back up.

"She dead?" he said as his eyes popped open.

"You better believe it!"

"You're a good friend, Rolly."

"Thanks. So are you."

"I got too close."

"Sometimes we do," I said.

A Mask of Glass

Maddie McLeod

Crack.

A mask of glass serves to protect; protect me from the torrential bullets of the devil's almighty machine gun.

Crack.

A mask of glass serves to protect; protect me from the grenade which my closest yet treacherous friend throws in my path.

Crackle.

A mask of glass serves to protect; protect me from the razor-edged swords that masked strangers wield, claiming they know who I am.

Crack, crack.

A mask of glass serves to protect.; protect me from the scalding flames society ignites around my family, my home, myself.

Crack, crackle, crack.

Snap.

Smash.

A mask of glass serves to protect; protect me from the jagged shard now lodged in my cheek, blood seeping from my skin.

Squelch.

A mask of glass serves to protect; protect me from the world, but not from myself.

Crunch.

A mask of glass serves to destroy.

Seasonal Greeting—Molly Satterthwaite

PSYCHOBABBLE, TOIL AND TROUBLE

Stephen McQuiggan

There are no monsters anymore. Not real ones. Only sad little men who hack and kill, the serial bores who claim the title 'monster' by default. They have no artistry, no romance. Not like the vampire.

But the vampires are all gone.

Wiped out by the AIDS virus, their centuries old blood swilling antics cruelly halted by one infected tot too many. Their population dwindled to a few undead corpses decaying slowly in Rumanian rest homes, measuring time by the rattle of their fetid breath, each exhalation a rustle of the bat wings they once soared on.

The werewolves have grown domesticated. Where once they ravaged young maidens on foggy moors by the light of Mother Moon, now they are content to lie by the fireside, their pelts scratched by drunken masters whilst they dream of fetching sticks. Their lycanthrope lethargy has rendered them toothless and cuddly.

The Mummies, those bandaged spirits of the noble Pharaohs, have simply given up. Evicted and robbed of their mystery by archaeologists, their sacred homes crushed under the feet of a million gawping tourists. Technology has left them behind, and the grunge look is so old hat. They belong in a museum. Their hearts are dust.

Technology got the Creature too. Interstate 151 runs right over the Black lagoon now. No more screaming virgins will be carried into that murky swamp.

Frankenstein's Monster, ashamed and embarrassed by his ever more comic portrayal in the media, got plastic surgery, liposuction, and a full body wax. He lives in Wyoming now where he runs a gas station and the locals call him Big Al.

Even the poor old phantom has come a cropper, the economic downturn has seen opera audiences plummet.

One by one, science has destroyed them all; the science of disbelief. A science that renamed Jekyll and Hyde schizophrenia, that turned the ghosts of our nightmares into badly developed photographs.

All that is apart from Amelia Liverwort, last of the witches.

A hideous crone, her skin green of hue, she lived in a cottage in the very darkest part of the forest. Stroking her black cat, her broomstick primed by her cauldron, she would cackle maniacally at tales of her kinds' demise.

Although she got most of her ingredients for her wicked spells from The Body Shop, and although the black gown and pointed hat she habitually wore were Miss Selfridge originals, she was a witch nonetheless, bringing down doom on all who strayed past her quaint little house.

But alas, there lay the crux of her dilemma, for very few ever did.

Gone were the carefree days of family picnics in the woods. People were more wary now, and preferred the plastic sanctuary of McDonalds or Burger King; a slower variation of the death she would have given them. So she sat home watching daytime TV, growing ever more shocked at the debauchery of the outside world.

She may have been a vicious old hag with a penchant for boiled infants but she considered herself a modern woman and little by little guilt set in. Very soon the need to confess her sins outweighed the need to bake hemlock and schoolboy pie.

She rang a few morning chat show phone-ins but was dismissed as a crank, and her letters to the tabloid problem pages never did get published. She couldn't blame them, she supposed, her ilk had become figures of fun in today's society, cartoon-like and safe. Halloween had become commercialised and sanitised; like a wax apple, it looked the same but left a bad taste in the mouth.

Amelia made up her mind to consult a psychiatrist. She had heard them referred to as 'head shrinkers' and thought this strange; it had taken her three centuries to master *that* spell.

Dr Levers was a spindly little man whose joints creaked every time he spoke. His probing questions slid expertly over the wet slugs of his lips, slaloming freely through the maze of her tortured mind. But his eyes rarely left his watch, his special watch, the one that counted out large amounts of money every forty minutes.

Amelia, green as envy in a room of pale lime, appeared to have sucked the very colour from the walls. She told him of her upbringing, of her father Satan and her mother the wolf. She told him of her sister who had lured Hansel and Gretel to her chocolate house, and how the press had lied saying the brats had pushed her into an oven - the cheek of it!

They had eaten them at a family get-together, one of the last as it had turned out, before several of her aunts had moved to Salem and discovered the locals there preferred their stakes burnt.

For weeks she went, the good doctor only listening, never judging as she poured out her black heart. With the heavy canopies of his eyelids never blinking, and his chin permanently resting on the sinuous pyramid of his fingers, he looked like a statue named Understanding.

But one day, one glorious stormy rain swept day, as Amelia parked her broom by his studiously empty desk Dr Levers announced, 'Amelia my dear, I have made an important breakthrough.'

He ushered her to the faux leather couch and positioned himself above her, speaking in the authoritative voice of God.

'None of this is your fault, you are not to blame!'

'I'm not?' Amelia was incredulous, this guy was good, really good, worth every penny she had intimidated out of those pensioners. She felt better already.

'Of course not! I've been studying your case notes and you fall right into the category I suspected from the outset.'

'You mean, I'm not a monster?' Amelia scratched voraciously at a herd of warts she had stabled under her armpit. 'There are others like me?'

Dr Levers laughed a humourless, patronising laugh. 'Miss Liverwort, I am afraid your condition is depressingly common nowadays.'

Amelia's chin, already visible to her own yellow eyes, jutted out even further, the iron bristles that sprouted there causing the good doctor to recline further back in his Parker Knoll.

'Really? I thought I was different somehow. I was convinced I was a manifestation of pure undiluted evil.'

'No, no, no. Trust me, your looks would induce nausea in the stoutest constitution but that does not mean you are wicked.'

'But all those things I told you…'

'You were merely the catalyst for those events, they were beyond your control. It's interesting you referred to your father as the devil himself; a vital clue to your present state of mental turmoil. This suggests to my razor sharp and highly trained mind,' he pointed a bony knuckle in the general direction of a photocopied certificate that hung by the door, 'that your father conjures up bad memories that you have suppressed. You have never had any children of your own, and by your own admission have had difficulties forming lasting relationships.'

'But what have I suppressed? What terrible secrets have I hidden away all these years that have driven me to carry out such abnormal acts?'

'Your father was abusive towards you as a child, hence your violence towards children now. It is a vicious cycle, the abused becomes the abuser. Text book stuff really. So you see Amelia, you are not wicked, quite the reverse. Because you loved your parents so much you never believed they could hurt you, and when they did you just couldn't accept it. You blamed yourself.'

25

'It's all mummy and daddy's fault?'

'Trust me, all your sins, no matter how heinous, rest squarely on the inadequate shoulders of your parents. If you ask me, they want locking up.'

Amelia left him, happier than she had been since she started that fire in London and told the police a cow had done it, and returned to her little cottage.

'Monsters indeed!' laughed Dr Levers smugly as he hopped off his chair after a fly, blissfully unaware he was now a toad.

Amelia swapped her cape and her broomstick for a cardigan and a tartan trolley and became just another bitter, nosey old woman. Now all the monsters really are gone and we are left with only our own evil.

Dig out your B movies and shed a tear at their passing.

Dark Spaces—Jay Duret

To Stop a Monster

Don Ford

Recipe to stop a monster
Now listen carefully for sure
Pick a night of a bright full moon
There it is, that big hairy buffoon

Clumsy lumbering fool is he
It hides behind some big old tree
Then scares the children and runs away
Hides in the darkest woods, so they say

But on this night you can set your trap
You will catch this creature in a snap
We want to catch it in its antics
It's just a matter of semantics

Returns once more to the crime scene then
Like a crook or burglar comes again
Pour glue in its footsteps, it'll be back
You will stop this monster in his tracks

Swamp Creature—Don Ford

Blood or Chocolate—Molly Satterthwaite

Lullabye

J.D. Smith

No monster lives beneath the bed.
He likes to stay out in the shed.
But if you want something to dread
I'll get/find a ghoul, or troll, instead.

The Cat Who Broke the Witch's Heart

Sephonē Zorro

Illustrations by Jane Gregoritch and Sephonē Zorro

Once upon a time a young woman named Agnes moved to Nova Scotia. There she lived in a modest seaside cottage with a small cowshed and garden off the side. It wasn't long before she married. Her husband, Robert, was a merchant sea captain. His ship sailed from a small harbor a short walk down the hill.

The young couple was soon delighted to have a baby girl, Bonnie, but the captain had to spend much time away at sea, and when alone the young mother began to fear that her baby might be stolen, especially at night. Some town girl might be jealous, but mostly Agnes feared the sand gnomes, evil little sprites that lived in the dunes. Sand gnomes love causing mischief by stealing folks' most precious things. This was famously true on the rough golf course that ran there along the coast. Many a golfer swore it was sand gnomes that had stolen his balls when he couldn't find them. Agnes just knew that sand gnomes were sure to steal such a cute, precious little baby as her Bonnie, if they possibly could.

So it was that Agnes went to town to buy a cat. She soon found one, but not just any cat, for this cat was said to be a true Scottish *cat sith*, a kind of very large black cat with a white spot on its chest, a very long tail—an animal traditionally believed to be magical. His name was Malcolm Macfluff.

Agnes brought Malcolm home, gave him a nice saucer of warm milk fresh from the cow outside, then took him into the nursery to meet Baby Bonnie. The baby cooed as Malcolm curled up beside her. Agnes explained that it would be Malcolm's job to guard Bonnie, especially at night when the sand gnomes were about.

"That I will surely do, Madam," said Malcolm Macfluff, lifting his head, for being a *cat sith*, and magical, he understood Human quite well—though, the truth be told, he suspected that people often didn't hear right what he said to them.

Malcolm was quite taken with Mistress Agnes, and soon figured she must be a witch—a very good witch, assuredly—but one in hiding by appearing to lead a conventional life, "fitting in" with the village. This was undoubtedly necessary as common folk were likely to misunderstand all mystical spirits, good as well as bad. How did Malcolm know she was a witch? Well, besides being a *cat sith* himself, and thus having a natural affinity for other beings of the magical gifts (indeed, some even still maintain that *cats sith* themselves are witches, but that is pure poppycock), Baby Bonnie was so enchanting that Malcolm knew her mother had to be one of magical breeding.

Yes, this would be quite a nice job, living incognito in the service of a being similar to himself; but Malcolm would have been grateful to get any position, as times were very bad then back in dear old Scotland. Besides, guard duty fit his military background.

Malcolm had had his life of military service cut short just recently when the pipe and drum unit of his battalion of the Royal Highland Regiment was transferred to Canada for a tour, and the English Sargent-Major Music Director decided that they would forgo the traditional *cat sith* mascot for a slobbering Newfoundland dog. The very day they landed in Nova Scotia the bloody fool Englishman dumped Lance Corporal Macfluff without ceremony at the same shop where he bought the stupid dog. At least he'd left the small wooden trunk with Macfluff's kit in it. It went with his purchase.

That night, right before bedtime, Agnes showed Malcolm a little crooked heart-shaped pin as she placed it on the baby's blanket.

"Now this, Mr. Macfluff, is what is called a 'witch's heart'. It once belonged to my own dear mother, and hers before that. Scottish mothers put them on the wee baby so that bad spirits, like those nasty little sand gnomes, will know that this baby has stolen a heart, in this case mine, and if they try in any way to hurt her, they will have the wrath of a most angry witch of a mother to deal with."

"Of course! I knew it!" Macfluff thought to himself, but what he said out loud was just, "Very well, Madam," though, as often, he was not sure he was understood.

It must be said that Malcolm thought the witch's heart thing totally unnecessary, what with him on guard. But still, the pin was pretty. It was made of fine Sterling silver with small red garnets encrusted along the rim, but with a larger one at the top, the "root" of the heart. Malcolm especially liked the little crook at the heart's end, signifying that of a witch. Why witches have crooks in their hearts he did not know, but whatever the shape of her heart, Mistress Agnes seemed very sweet, and most Scottish—save for her accent, which was a soft, clear Canadian.

That night Malcolm settled down again next to Bonnie, and fell asleep.

"*Pssst*, Cat!"

What was that? Macfluff opened his sleepy eyes and looked out the window. There in the moonlight, with its doughy face pressed against the window glass, was a little man barely a foot high dressed in raggedy brown pants and a short, dirty waistcoat, standing up on a stump to look in.

"How much do you want for that baby?" whispered the sand gnome.

"Off with you!" hissed Macfluff. "Guarding the wee baby is me duty. Scots, especially us *cats sith*, the most fearsome of all the world's domestic felines, take our duties as most sacred. If you come in here, I'll shred your puny body to bloody strips, then spit out the bones before swallowing the stink'n meat of you!" Malcolm had practiced that threat while in training for the Royal Highland Regiment. He was sure it would scare the dickens out of a little sand gnome.

"Well suit yourself, Cat, but I am Pugsley, Chief of all the sand gnomes, and I have much you may want. I even have a tin of very nice sardines right here, right now," said the sand gnome.

Malcolm thought he detected a cockney English accent, and it raised his blood to a near boil.

"Off with ya, ya sandy scum! I'll not be bought!" he hissed, but quietly, not wanting to awaken the baby.

In the morning, all was well. Young mother Agnes had gotten the kind of good night's sleep that a new mother rarely has, for Baby Bonnie had slept soundly all night.

"Yes, Madam, there was a sand gnome about here last night, but you need not worry, for a hundred of them stink'n rats would be no match for a *cat sith* trained as a soldier of Her Majesty's Royal Highlanders."

Although she said nothing in response to his report, Agnes poured Malcolm another nice saucer of warm milk, petted and stroked his head, then let him out of the cottage to roam the village during the day. It was a pleasant little place, and Malcolm soon made friends with some old fishermen down by the dock, and even got a fish head. He had hoped for more, he had to admit, but all the fisher folk here were clearly Scotsmen by heritage, and more than a wee bit stingy. Still he reflected again on how hard life was in Scotland, and considered himself fortunate.

That night, the sand gnome came again to the window, and offered to buy the baby anew, now for two cans of sardines. As before, Malcolm sent him off, this time with a louder growl, and a longer curse.

Still, the sand gnome kept coming, night after night. Malcolm saw this as a great bother, but not much of a threat. If that little man, Pugsley, barely a foot high, ever came in the house, Malcolm would dispatch him with one quick bite to the back of the neck, then drag his limp, stinking body to the docks to feed to the seagulls. So there!

To back his threat up, Malcolm showed Pugsley a toothy snarl, flexed his claws, and lashed his tail.

Nevertheless, the sand gnome was not deterred in his persistence.

"Listen, Cat," Pugsley began differently one night, "you won't sell me the baby, even though I'd take very good care of her and pay you well to boot. OK, clearly I'm wasting my time pursuing that. But how about dealing on something else?

Malcolm stared back at him in stony silence.

"You see," continued the gnome, "I am charmed by this child, and would miss her very much if I didn't see her every night. That's why I keep coming back and stay for many hours each time, despite your very rude, and I must add, unjustified threats. But if I had something to remind me of her, say that little heart pin on her blanket, maybe I could just look at that instead.

"How about this? If each night, right after Mistress Agnes goes to sleep, you'd just lend me that pin, I could take it home to look at all night long, then bring it back before dawn when the mother awakens. She'll never know, and of course with you on guard the baby will be just as safe without the little trinket. There would be a full can of fine North Sea kippered herrings for you each night. What do you say?"

Kippers, a whole can of kippers every night. Malcolm did love kippers, very, very much. Hadn't had 'um in years, though. Times were way too hard in Scotland now for a cat to get any kippers.

Malcolm thought about it. It was certainly true that the pin didn't add to his charge's safety, what with him there. It was even a bit insulting—unintended, of course, by his dear Mistress Agnes—to suggest that anything beyond his vigilance was needed. And the sand gnome would give him lovely kippers just to hold that insignificant little blanket bauble at night. Still…

"It's true this pin is needless with me on guard, but my mistress believes it very important, as it signifies that her own heart is set upon her Baby Bonnie. If I loan you the pin one night, and you don't bring it back by dawn, what will I do?"

"Oh, Sir Cat, you don't have to worry about that," said the sand gnome. "I'll bring it back. You have a Sand Gnome's Word of Honor!"

"*Hoot, mon!*" called out Malcolm, "It's not because of that that I'm not worried. I'm not worried because if you don't I'll sniff out your stinking sand gnome shanty in them dunes, catch all of your accursed sand gnome kin, then boil them all alive to make me that night's dinner of barley, carrot and gnome-tripe soup. All except for you, Pugsley, you miserable imp. You, you I'll boil your miserable, wretched, rotten, smelly, infernal, vermin stomach right before you while you still live to see it to make me a haggis, a haggis that I'll then feed to crazed, starving wharf rats, as nothing else would touch the putrid thing! Your head I'll then toss to the crabs, who will chew on it into all screaming eternity, as you, Pugsley, will surely feel it as you languish in unspeakable misery in the depths of darkest hell forever!" Malcolm was quite proud of that last threat; he'd just made it up.

41

So the agreement was struck. Malcolm unpinned the witch's heart from Baby Bonnie's blanket, opened the window an inch, and pushed it under the sash to the sand gnome, who at the same time slid over to him a can of kippers, already peeled open.

The sand gnome left, and Malcolm shut the window tight and locked it. He ate all the lovely kippers, then snuggled back down by the baby, smelling, he thought pleasantly, of nice smoked fish.

The next thing he knew, the sun was shining in through the window. Baby Bonnie was sleeping soundly, but Pugsley hadn't returned with the pin. Malcolm feared for what Agnes would think. But maybe she'd think it just came off and was somewhere in the room…? Yes, while Agnes looked for it, Malcolm could be out and about and find that accursed sand gnome, who would pay sorely for not keeping his word. Malcolm would then bring the pin back and drop it in a place where mother would soon find it. Yes, that plan would work... it must. Have to remember to trash the kipper can, though. He'd do it on the way out to the shore.

But Agnes didn't come in. Malcolm waited in the bedroom, and waited. Bonnie was restless, wanting breakfast, and her mother.

Finally Malcolm pawed open the door to the bedroom. He walked from room to room, but no one was there. He opened the front door, and there saw what were clearly the footprints of Mistress Agnes, following those of little boots.

Malcolm knew immediately what had happened. Pugsley had stolen the witch's heart—Agnes's heart—so she had had to follow him.

Dear, sweet, Scottish Agnes! The best mistress a *cat sith* could ever hope to have, and the mother of the precious Baby Bonnie, his sacred charge! Oh, fool, fool him, accursed Malcolm! He had not seen the ruse for his gluttony—and his pride! The shame, the bloody, intolerable shame of it all! He'd been hornswoggled of his most sacred honor for but a can of fish by a bloody cockney-in-Canada, stink'n sand gnome!

This must not stand. This would not stand! He so swore not only on Clan Macfluff's Sacred Highlands Holy Honor, but especially on that of his most venerable ancestor, Archibald Macfluff I, first King of Cats of All Scotland, one who, like him, had proudly displayed the white chest markings of a *cat sith* warrior! Every bit of such sacred honor he was now hell-bent on reclaiming. He'd make it all aright, or perish in the attempt! So did he then cry while on his knees, tears streaming from his eyes.

First, however, he got Baby Bonnie a bottle of warm honey in water, laid her gently back in her crib, and locked her in her room after assuring himself that the window was locked securely, too. She would be safe; he would not be gone long, and at the villain's throat at that.

Then he went to his wooden chest. There they were, beneath the cat bedding and the boxes of catnip he had sworn off for his health years ago. He pulled on his tartan kilt, fastened his bonny Scottish dirk to his belt, hid the smaller *sgian-dubh* under his left arm, and hung a small shield, the *targe*, to his front. Finally, he secured his sturdy *claidhmor*—the great basket-hilt sword—to its hanger, and set his cap aright. Pulling the *claidhmor* from its sheath, it gleamed in the sunlight, for at all times Malcolm Macfluff had kept it clean, well-oiled, and sharp.

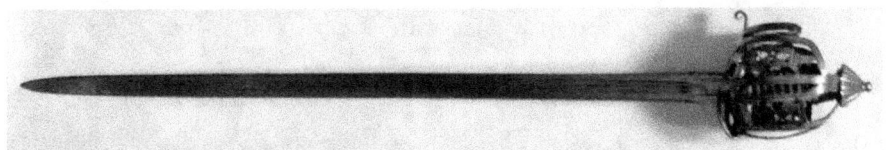

Clan Macfluff sword, circa 1706. Photo by Sephonē Zorro

He set off, following the clear trail toward the shore.

It wasn't far into the dune lands when he came to the rundown shanty where the grubby clan of sand gnomes lived. He yalled his most chilling Highlands yall, drew his sword, and prepared to charge, when the door opened.

Out walked Agnes, cradling Pugsley like a child. The gnome wore the silver and garnet witch's heart pin upon his chest. Agnes was clearly in a deep trance. Malcolm raised his sword.

"Unhand her, you fiend!' he roared.

"Well, if it isn't my good friend Malcolm. A pleasure to see you on this fine morning, Pussy Cat," the sand gnome called out, waving. "Malcolm, I'd like you to meet some of my relatives."

At this a dozen other foot-tall men marched out of the shanty and stood behind Pugsley. Each held an iron club stolen off the golf course as a weapon three times longer than he was high.

"They've all come to meet my new wife, Agnes. Oh, by the way, we'd appreciate you being a good boy, Malcolm, by bringing our baby over, right now."

Malcolm saw that he now faced an overwhelming foe. He stood frozen, but not from fear, for fear is not an emotion known to a Highlands *cats sith*. He was thinking.

"Yes, surely you now have me overpowered, Pugsley," he said after a while. "I will not part a mother from her child, no matter how despicable the man with whom she now is. I must leave it to the captain, her true husband, to deal with your wickedness when he returns. I will go and get the baby."

"Wise of you, cat," said the sand gnome. "By the way, we'll be long gone before that fool Captain Kelpie returns. You should stay here with him and keep him company, for you are both silly fools."

Macfluff stifled his rage as he ran back to the cottage. There, in a fine bag of Shetland wool at the very bottom of his chest it rested—a set of Highlands pipes. It was small, being cat-sized, but he knew that with his determination it would surely do what needed doing. He clutched it with one arm, and holding Baby Bonnie with the other, marched double-time back to the shanty in the dunes.

"Here's the blessed baby," Malcolm said as he put Bonnie gently on the ground. Still in a trance, Agnes moved toward her while still carrying the evil Pugsley in her arms. The armed sand gnome rabble stayed at the ready with their clubs and growled.

Then Malcolm Macfluff positioned his Great Highlands Pipes.

With the same wail that had once shaken the glens, moors, heath, and even the very lochs, Lance Corporal Malcolm Macfluff, recently of Her Majesty's Royal Highland Regiment, let blast with the most fearsome—and out of tune—of all the great Scottish battle marches, *The Black Bear*. The sand gnomes all screamed, dropped their weapons, and held their ears as they rolled in agony on the ground. The baby cried. Even in her trance, Agnes wept—but for joy at hearing the Great Pipes, for she was, whether witch or not, a most true Scott, just as the loyal cat had always known. Then, suddenly, as Malcolm Macfluff, a learned as well as magical *cat sith* after all, had planned, the little witch's heart on Pugsley's chest fell to the ground. The sharp notes of the Great Pipes had cut it clean in two.

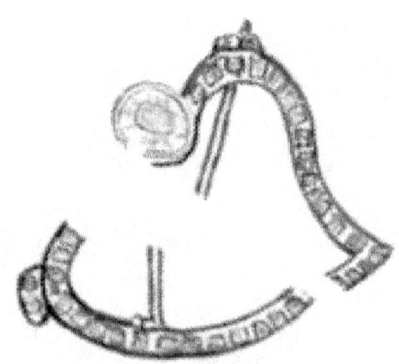

Agnes snapped out of the evil spell. Realizing immediately what had happened, she threw Pugsley down hard on the ground, and ran for her baby. With a lusty cheer, Malcolm then drew his sword anew, launched a terrifying one-cat Highlands Charge, and chased all the screaming sand gnomes into the cold, dark North Atlantic Ocean. They were last seen in Boston Harbor, hundreds of miles to the south, bobbing up and down, covered in filth.

That very afternoon Captain Robert returned. There was great rejoicing.

"What a fine and most brave kitty you are, Mr. Malcolm Macfluff," he said. "We are eternally grateful for having rid us of those vermin, and proud to have you as a member of our family."

Although Malcolm Macfluff was clearly the hero of the family, the noble cat, now as honest as he was fierce and canny, told the full truth about what had happened, and hung his head in abject shame. Despite his new family's protests, he refused any reward of the many fresh fish they offered him, even the finest smoked wild Scottish salmon.

Instead, right then and there, Macfluff reduced himself one full step in rank from Lance Corporal to Private, and for all his days thereafter insisted on wearing the broken witch's heart, bound back together with a strip of old reed taken from his pipes, on the front of his cap. It was ever a reminder to him of how close a moment's gluttony and disregard for duty had come to breaking several hearts, including his own, forever.

For the rest of his life Malcolm Macfluff dedicated himself to the loyal service of his new North American family, even in the face of death. From such would come many a grand and honorable adventure…of which all the world will learn, in due time.

Archibald Macfluff
Brave King of Noble Cats

Ancient Armorial of Archibald I,
First King of Cats for All of Scotland
(Discovered by Sephonē Zorro in the Clan Macfluff Archives, Inverness, Scotland.)

Goblin Stew

By Matthew J. Barbour

Listen close, a recipe for you,
The witches call it, goblin stew.

Begin with cauldron, water hot,
Add these ingredients to your pot:

Eye of newt, leg of frog,
Whisker of cat, tail of dog,

Horse mane, cow utter,
Rat brain, whale blubber
Slugs, snails, handful of ivy,
Beetles and worms extra grimy,

Goat intestines mashed into paste,
A pinch of nettles, toadstools for taste,

Toss in some mud and mossy brick,
Stir it with an old oak stick,

Let it simmer for an hour or two,
Then gobble up some goblin stew.

The Tadpole

J.D. Smith

The tadpole grew two pairs of legs
And hopped across the road.
By the time he missed his tail,
He'd turned into a toad.

Snail Slime Whine

By Kelly Bakshi

Sally Snail whined, "I don't like my slime.

I feel yucky all of the time."

She slid to the doctor. "What should I do?"

The doctor advised, "Nothing, the slime brings out the shine in you."

"That's nice," said the determined Sally.

"But I want it off." So, she slid down a dark alley!

She met a witch with a magic wand.

Sally's wish was granted. Her slime was gone.

"Hooray!" cheered Sally, beaming with pride,

Forgetting she *needed* her slime to slide.

Her skin began to crack and peel.

She started to cry. "How sad I feel!

I should've been proud to be who I am.

Then, I would not be stuck in this jam."

Her tears wet her body and made her slick.

Her slime returned nice and thick.

"There's only one me and I'm going to shine!"

And that was the end of her snail slime whine.

Worm of Wisdom—Tevin Hansen

Sci-fi Haiku

Denny Marshall

no news of landing
alien party all lost
in vacuum cleaner

"you can have rover"
Martian parents said to son
when battery dies

aliens ponder
what do humans call earthworms?
on other planets

helium breathing
aliens that visited
sure did talk funny

aliens laughing
about Earths tallest building
their cell tower size

A Clock's Work

Sophia Whittemore

The time of man is never very long, not when you look at the grand scheme of time. Man's time is kept by a grandfather clock, silent and towering, made of black ivory with gears that gnash and a pendulum which cries murder in the dark of night. The times on the clock are kept by the hour, lined up in a hall that stretches up, out, and over, but never back.

Never has time gone back.

Greta, an old spinster woman, tends to all the clocks. She can often be found walking, always forward, in the endless hall. Her skeletal hands, though arthritic, never waver, not while they have so much to do. Down the hall, you can hear the shadows whisper, their fears ignited as their hearts beat towards death:

"She never actually fixes the clocks."

"She kills *them."*

The last clock she struck was old and crotchety, with all manner of scales and claws and fangs protruding from it. She'd put a stop to that one by taking up a rock and smashing the whole lot to kingdom come.

She's slow and she's old, but she sees fairly well. She smiles, for just three clocks away is the proud, grandfather clock of man.

She's almost there, just about. She's so close now at the end of the hall. She can see her brother taking up his job to make newer, brighter clocks. She relishes the chance to destroy these clocks, as well, but that chance may never come. And even if it did, that task would be nearly impossible. For her brother's clocks are made of better stuff: starlight and laughter and broken dreams and such. They're too shiny to destroy.

Certain clocks were never destroyed. Some were merely paused for a bit, only to start up again when their times had come. Some clocks died natural deaths, while others died gruesome ones. And still man's has yet to number among any of them—at least, the ones of importance.

Now, two clocks away lies man's time to come. Impatient now, old Greta makes her way to its ebony flanks and gazes up at the clock face. The hands pause and begin to tremble under the weight of her heavy stare, its pendulum screams so loud it cries.

The old spinster huffs and mutters, "No, this will not do."

She reaches within the folds of her raggedy skirt and brings out a silver key. Like a dagger past a heartstring, she reaches in with the key and cranks the clockwork back once, then twice. Satisfied, the clock sighs in content, pendulum freshly oiled and gears gone silent. Greta returns to her job, puttering aimlessly after her brother, who seems to grow younger with every century that his sister ages. He'll be a babe again before they know it, and she'll be dead!

No matter for us. Since the clock of humanity has been wound tight again, we can carry on as normal, eh? And all because Greta, and she alone, allowed it tick for one more year. And yet...

She's starting to get mighty sick of it.

One Afternoon

J.D. Smith

I sat cross-legged in a field
For an hour or two, or four.
My feet went numb and fell asleep—
And then began to snore.

"I worry about headwinds," he said.

Headwinds—Jay Duret

Dad Goes Bald

J.D. Smith

His hair
Flies here and there,
In patches where
He still has hair.

In other spots, his head is bare,
His scalp out in the open air.
His head's sunburned—he needs a cap to wear.

In the morning, he looks into the mirror, where
He wonders, while he was in bed, did someone tear
Out more of his hair.

"It isn't fair! It isn't fair!"
He says with great despair.

So if you care,
And have some hair
To spare,
Please share.

Authors, Poets, and Illustrators

Monica Adrian is an artist and writer born on Halloween. She graduated from CSUN with a Bachelors degree in English/Creative Writing.

Elle Alexander is a woman with a highly active imagination. She lives in Michigan where she continues to write twisted tales and dream dreams of marvelous things. You can find out more about her latest novel, *Grimly Jane*, on Facebook.

Kelly Bakshi is a freelance writer and childrens book author. She lives in Rye, New York with her husband and two sons. While she has never met a meowing dog, she would love to train a bunny to behave as a house cat.

Matthew J. Barbour is a speculative fiction author living with his wife and three children in Bernalillo, New Mexico. When he is not writing fiction, Mr. Barbour manages Jemez Historic Site and contributes to a number of regional newspapers, including the *Red Rocks Reporter* and the *Sandoval Signpost*.

Scáth Beorh is the author of the story collections *Children & Other Wicked Things* (JWK Fiction), *Always After Thieves Watch* (Wildside Press), and the MG novel *October House* (Emby Press, Oct 2014) as well as the forthcoming epistolary novel *Blood* (Emby, 2015). He lives with his wife Ember in a Folk Victorian carriage house on the Atlantic Coast.

Authors, Poets, and Illustrators cont.

Jay Duret is a San Francisco based writer and illustrator who blogs at www.jayduret.com. More than two dozen of Jay's stories have been published or are forthcoming in online and print journals, including *Narrative Magazine*, *Blue Fifth Review*, *Gargoyle* and *December*. Jay's first novel, *Nine Digits*, tells the story of 15 year-old Nee-Nee Marcus' quest to win $100 million on a reality TV contest. See the book trailer at www.ninedigits.com. Jay's illustrations are posted daily to Instagram @joefaces and twitter @jayduret.

Don Ford began at 15 to pen Poetry & Short Stories. He writes in every genre and hopes humor keeps readers turning the pages of his work. Don's work has landed him publishing contracts throughout the U. S. and Europe; Portugal and Cyprus in particular with connections in 62 other countries.

Jane Gregoritch is a pediatrician and geneticist. She is married to L. R. Baxter, and is the mother of Rhea Baxter, a frequent art contributor to *Stinkwaves Magazine*. She lives with them and horses, dogs, cats, and birds in Santa Fe, NM.

Tevin Hansen is the author of numerous books and short stories. He currently resides in Lincoln, Nebraska, where he enjoys skateboarding, reading half a dozen books simultaneously, and chasing his two small children around the house while singing horrendous versions of children's songs.

Denny E. Marshall has had art, poetry, and fiction published. One recent credit would be cover art for Disturbed Digest June 2015, the other half of the drawing is on the back cover. See more at www.dennymarshall.com

Authors, Poets, and Illustrators cont.

While finishing up her high school education, 17 year old **Maddie McLeod** loves to craft short stories that leave her readers craving more. She has been previously published in *Canvas Lit. Magazine* as well as *Cuckoo Quarterly*. She is also extremely grateful that *Stinkwaves Magazine* decided to take on her story.

Stephen McQuiggan liked nothing more than walking under ladders, breaking mirrors, and taunting magpies until he fell into a sudden and inexplicable coma. His first novel, *A Pig's View Of Heaven*, is available now from Grinning Skull Press.

Molly Satterthwaite is a recent college graduate with a BFA in illustration. She is currently a freelance artist and is creating children's book illustrations.

J.D. Smith's books include the picture book *The Best Mariachi in the World* and three collections of poetry for adults, most recently *Labor Day at Venice Beach*. He lives in Washington, DC with his wife Paula Van Lare, Roo the Rescue Dog, and two cats: Pantera and Mr. Clean.

Sophia Whittemore is an author of the Chicago area who has also won the Best Midwestern Writing award, first place in journalism and second in creative writing. She writes her characters based on inspiration from growing up as a half Indonesian with a Jewish heritage. She is a seventeen-year old currently attending Benet Academy. In her spare time, you can find her trying to get a novel published, relearning Hebrew, or attending DuPage Indonesian Association cultural events.

Sephonē Zorro is the author of many fairy tales, myths, children's stories, and poems. Along with her twin, the comic and social satirist, The Rt. Rev. Dr. Art Bupkis, she is a literary ward of L.R. Baxter.

Thank You's

As always, we want to thank our very talented contributors for another great issue. Without them there would be no Stinkwaves. If you would like to be a part of our accomplished crew, visit www.stinkwavesmagazine.com for submission guidelines, or email us at submissions@stinkwavesmagazine.com with any questions.

Follow us on Facebook and Twitter to stay up to date on the latest Stinkwaves shenanigans.

Handersen Publishing is an independent publishing house.

We hope you enjoyed this issue and will consider supporting our many talented contributors by leaving a review on Amazon.

Thank you.

Handersen Publishing
www.handersenpublishing.com

More Young Adult, Middle Grade, and Picture Books from our talented contributors:

Black Fox In Thin Places Scáth Beorh, Emby Press, Middle Grade
   The Tolkien-esque adventures of Sionnach Varela, a 17th Century Irish girl who seemingly stumbles upon a noble denizen of that country's most famous folk, the Sidhe.

The Best Mariachi in the World by J.D. Smith and Dani, Delta Publishing Company: Raven Tree Press, Picture Book
   Everyone in Gustavo's family is in a mariachi band. Everyone except Gustavo, that is. They all play violínes, trompetas and guitarrones. Gustavo would love to join the band, but he can't play any of the instruments. This book is available in English–only, Spanish–only or embedded (English with Spanish sprinkled throughout) editions.

The First Americans by Kelly Bakshi, Guardian Angel Publishing, Inc., Middle Grade
   Would you use a buffalo bladder as a canteen or wear a coat made out of seal skin? Native Americans cleverly used everything in their environment in order to survive.

Grimly Jane by Elle Alexander, Oliver Press LLC, Middle Grade
   Jane Worthington is an orphan who has been cruelly treated by everyone. When one day she is locked away as usual, she discovers a secret door to another world. Crawling through it, she begins a mysterious and exciting journey that will change her life forever.

Mr. Boggarty the Halloween Grump by Tevin Hansen, Handersen Publishing, Middle Grade
   Trixie Cole and her friends are determined to teach Mr. Boggarty a lesson in Halloween etiquette. Little did they know that it would be them learning the true meaning of Halloween.

Mummy Mouse by Tevin Hansen, Handersen Publishing, YA
   Eleven year old C.K. has a secret. An epic secret with a furry white coat, long tail, four scratchy feet...and a sickening desire to drain enough life-forces to become a Pharaoh, a mouse-god, and seek his revenge on the two-legged world.

<u>Myth-Busting Columbus</u> by Kelly Bakshi, Guardian Angel Publishing, Inc., Middle Grade

Columbus convinced royals to fund his voyage; he forged new water routes and introduced Europe to a new world. He also lied to his crew, murdered and enslaved Native Americans and never realized where in the world he actually was. You decide, is he a hero or a villain?

<u>Nine Digits</u> by Jay Duret, Second Wind Publishing, Middle Grade

Nee-Nee Marcus is a headstrong, self-absorbed, 15-year-old who despises her family. She would do anything to be free of them. When she hears about a new reality television program that will award a prize of $100 million, she decides she'll do whatever it takes to win. www.ninedigits.com.

<u>She Dreamed of Dragons</u> by Elizabeth J. M. Walker, Mirror World Publishing, YA

Trina is a dragon mage in a kingdom ruled by witches and wizard. In an effort to find a suitable teacher to help control her fire powers, she enters The Royal Tourney – a competition to find the next successor to the throne!

<u>Shonim</u> by Giulietta Spudich, YA

Sarah is bored at her family's summer home in the countryside, until she discovers a fairy in her garden. Despite her family's disbelief and the fairy tribe's fear, they become fast friends. Books I-V free on Bibliotastic.

<u>The Truth About Snails</u> by JD DeHart, Poetry

Ordinary objects take on a new form, and myths become real and move next door in the verses contained in this poem collection. Much of the writing was inspired by comic books and science fiction, and on concepts beyond the scope of the real world, and cast firmly in the supernatural.

<u>When I was a Grown-up</u> by Nichole Hansen, Handersen Publishing, Picture Book

A collection of silly poetry. These humorous rhymes and colorful illustrations will keep children and adults laughing.

www.ingramcontent.com/pod-product-compliance
Lightning Source LLC
Chambersburg PA
CBHW071204130626
46555CB00004B/1575